**THIS JOURNAL
BELONGS TO**

....

....

DATE

....

Triumphant Journal

written by
Theo & Anita Teow

ACKNOWLEDGEMENTS

We would firstly like to thank God for allowing us to create this journal. He is the centre of our lives and marriage and we hope that if you don't already know Him personally that you will experience Him through this book! If you do know Him personally, we hope this journal enriches your faith and marriage.

Secondly, we would like to thank our parents (Augustine, Susan, Ken, Angela, Lisa, Kevin) for their constant love and support - we wouldn't be the people we are today without you.

Thirdly, thank you to our mentors and friends Matt & Sofia, David & Inez. We love you all dearly and want to thank you for all the wisdom, advice and care you have selflessly poured into us. We certainly stand on the shoulders of giants!

Lastly, thank you so much to our friends Lillian and Sam for the artwork, formatting and styling of this journal. You have helped us make our simple draft into a beautiful book. Thank you so much!

Introduction

CONGRATULATIONS!
YOU'VE TAKEN THE LEAP.

You're about to take your marriage to the next level. But first, let us introduce ourselves. Our names are Theo and Anita; just before you ask where Simon and Alvin are (from the Chipmunks), ha ha. Very funny. Also, Anita is not just an Indian name, though it's incredibly popular there from what we hear!

We are passionate about helping couples reach and exceed the potential for their relationship. Our relationship has had plenty of twists and turns, funny stories to tell, and battles fought. We have amazing stories of God's providence, testimonies of His healing, and lessons learned of His love in the short time we've been married. If you take one thing away from this journal, let it be that God should be a central part of your life together. His love is too good to exclude from your relationship. As you write your story in the weeks to come, we believe that God will show His grace, goodness, patience, and power to you both in a fresh new way as you turn to Him for guidance in the easy and the challenging times.

In fact, if you already know Jesus as your Lord and Saviour, the conversations you will have through this journal will make His love shine even brighter through your relationship. If you don't know Jesus yet, we want to encourage you to discover the Person and the character of Jesus, listen to His lessons of sacrificial love, and make a personal decision to follow Him. We believe that hope for eternity and strength for today centres around knowing Him.

OUR HOPE FOR YOU

If you're anything like us, you want to do this right. This relationship you have is the closest you've ever been to another human being and you're keen to make it the best it can be! You might be engaged - excited for the marriage to come and currently planning the wedding... You might be experiencing the butterflies of newly-minted love, sweetly remembering the weeks and months since you both said yes to being a couple... You might already be married with or without kids, looking to pursue your happily ever after.

In every case, we believe that with the right tools, the necessary conversations, and most importantly by the power of a good God, you will be equipped to take your relationship to the next level. We believe marital joy, excellent communication, bountiful forgiveness, and empowering grace are all within reach for every couple. It's why we wrote this journal! It is our sincere hope that through this 52-week journey together, you will both learn more about yourselves and each other, discover new levels of emotional intimacy, and grow together like never before. In this journal you will find a structure to build dreams together, be vulnerable with each other, and discover new ways to bless one another. We are so excited for you! In fact, this journal should be seen as a blank canvas on which you'll both write your story. We believe we're simply giving you a place and space to do so. Every couple has such a unique origin, journey, and destination that we want you to catalogue it for your later selves and even your children to read. We know that this process will be a blessing to you both individually and together.

Why 'Triumphant'?

/traɪˈʌm.fənt/
Adjective
Having won a battle or contest; victorious.

Cambridge Dictionary

Triumph. Victory. These are words describing battles, less so a marriage... but should they? Modern marriage is set in a difficult context. Australians are bombarded with marketing for discreet dating for married couples (take the promotion campaigns for Ashley Madison prior to 2015's catastrophic user data leak), highly sexualised content on mainstream television and social media, as well as exceedingly easy access to free and paid pornography of generic and exotic preferences; it's no wonder that the average divorce rate stands at 1.9 per 1000 Australians, which is a pretty way to describe a staggering 33% divorce rate (Australian Bureau of Statistics; Jain, 2007). Take a moment to think of all your married friends. Statistically, 1 in every 3 of those couples is going to end up in divorce. I don't know about you, but that stung us to our core. If we were to tell you that your skydiving parachute would fail 33% of the time, would you still take the leap?

In summary, to be married at this point in time is no joke. It's not all doom and gloom though! Equipped with knowledge of the gravity of the task at hand, we must prepare for marriage with the same rigour and enthusiasm as we do with work, university, or school. After all, you are in a lifelong relationship with your husband or wife; this extends way beyond a simple business partnership or a collaboration on a research paper. You are tied together by a marital bond that lasts a lifetime. The promises you made to each other are weighty and significant - you have left the protection of your parents' covering and chosen to become one flesh (Genesis 2:24). This bond does not happen by itself; rather, just like the first time you met and became friends, it is a bond you must actively cultivate. Auto-pilot is not an option. Knowing the forces assembled against fidelity, the marriage you have is therefore a battle for love that you must stand in triumphantly and together.

The most important tool in improving your marriage is communication. In fact, our lack of communication often leads to us overestimating our sense of agreement with our spouse about significant hot-button marital issues (Sillars, Pike, Jones, & Murphy, 1984). Communication is a powerful tool to help us reveal the unspoken differences between our perspectives in marriage. In fact, every relationship is unique in its specifics, contexts, and geography, yet the most commonly doled out relationship advice from well-meaning elders is:

Communication is key.

Why is this said so often? Is there a principle here that we can cultivate? The answer is absolutely yes. The problem is that those same well-meaning people rarely stop to explain why communication is important, or how to achieve it. In fact we believe so strongly in communication that it made its way into our definition of a successful relationship:

> "A successful relationship comprises two communicative individuals who achieve oneness of vision through intentional conversation."

Communication is a relational supercharger that will enrich and enhance your relationship. Without it, the both of you might dull yourselves with Netflix or the search for the cafe with the best smashed avo on toast, but you will never go far enough to scratch the relational itch that you feel. With it, your interactions have a spark and life to them that will activate new joy, passion, and excitement between the two of you.

Something has got to change. Perhaps that's the reason you decided to pick up this journal. Others might have found themselves in a stable, but static relationship. You know that there is a new level of depth and intimacy you want to explore with your significant other, but you don't know where to start. Wherever you are, know that communication is as important and good as you imagined it to be. The great news is that you can start feeding your relationship the good stuff right now.

SCAFFOLDING GROWTH: THE BUILDING PROJECT

The key to having effective, deep, and empowering communication is to know how to develop it. So many of our elders have stumbled through their own journeys in marriage and love, only reflecting after decades that their lives could have been much more joyful with more communication. They end up sharing the old adage about communication wistfully, almost as if to guide you to a treasure they cannot themselves possess.

We believe that the secret is for us all to build a relationship with healthy communicative habits. Imagine your relationship is a bowling lane and healthy communication is having bumper rails installed. This makes sure that the bowling ball of our relationship moves forward in the direction we want. We don't want the relationship to fall into the gutters of our maladaptive habits that we're so familiar with. In setting a better path for your relationship, a framework is essential - it makes sure that you have a stepwise structure to help you on your way to being effective communicators.

Let's put this another way: you've been building a habit of communication over months, years, or even decades that you'd like to improve on or completely overhaul. How is a man/woman able to unlearn or modify a long-term habit? Through clear and simple steps that can help them move from good to great. Just like a building that will eventually become a grand and beautiful house, the scaffolding of your house must be present to help you construct it well; we believe that this journey you are about to embark on will lead you to build the communicative house of your dreams!

BUILDING ISN'T ALWAYS FUN

Did you know that $100 invested monthly in a market index fund that tracks the Australian Stock Exchange (ASX) has the potential to produce $52,093 in 20 years? We live in a society that prioritises quick solutions to complex issues. We like the flashing lights, the highlight reels, the fancy events... but we don't like being the one laying out the red carpet, building the things worth highlighting, or organising events. How mundane must it have felt to deposit money for 20 years and not so much as shuffle it around for a long time? Surely there must be a flashier way to get rich, or so you might have thought. Society has convinced us that the time-tested traditions of consistency and good old grit have gone the way of the dodo - to extinction. Communication is much like investing a little bit over time, or seeding a fruitful crop in the field. Consistently applying it will produce an overwhelmingly positive effect in the long run.

One challenge we face as married couples is the tendency to want the complicated and convenient solution instead of a simple and effortful one. We believe that a successful marriage does not have to require a fancy solution. Here's an example: the plethora of weight-loss pills and electrical-shock products that claim to help you lose weight could be replaced by a simpler gradual reduction in calories over time. Why does the former idea appear more appealing?

We like to believe that the only thing holding us back from an ideal body is that we simply don't have the right product in hand. It removes personal responsibility and discipline from the equation and puts it firmly in the hand of that shiny new doohickey that promises the world. What if you took the reins of responsibility back from convenient products and started embracing simplicity? You remove your dependence on the external world and realise that the ingredients of a successful marriage have always been inside the both of you. Simplifying a process increases its effectiveness, reduces the points at which it can fail, and reduces the needless complexity that can cause additional stress and confusion. It's a recipe for marital success.

Another issue is that our intentions are way bigger than our behaviours. Just like starting to hit the gym in January ('new year, new me'), we find ourselves aborting the mission by Australia day (the end of the same month!). This is generally because consistency is not easy; 77% of resolution-keepers can maintain it for a week past New Year's Day, but only 19% hold to their resolutions after 2 years (Norcross & Vangarelli, 1999). We're conditioned to set our attention on the showy methods of attaining wealth, health, and success ('Did anything really happen unless it's on Instagram?'). True wealth, health, and success is often produced in the regular application of sound principles over time. This is why communication does its best work by - you guessed it - the consistent application of a good habit over time... Just like the weekly habit of journaling together.

How does a well-meaning, motivated couple beat the curve of resolution quitters? We have developed this journal to help you do just that. This is a resource that will enable you to build a strong relationship underpinned by transparency, vulnerability, and mutual giving. Journaling is helpful to fostering a culture of oneness that will keep you both anchored on God's love in the good times and bad. It is a crucial step in developing a marriage relationship that will stand the test of time.

ESSENTIAL ELEMENTS OF THE WEEKLY CATCH-UP

So what do you get with this journal? Truth be told, these are almost commonsensical in their simplicity. As stated before, perhaps this is exactly what it needs to be for the two of you. Without further ado:

PRAYER

The bedrock of a good marriage is the ability to talk to God about your collective and individual struggles. A relationship based only on two individuals will have a much rockier path simply because their movement is towards each other at the best of times, which will lead to a head-on collision. A relationship with God as the cornerstone will allow you both to move in the same direction, following God together. Inviting God into your relationship is as simple as praying, or talking to God. Open your time together with prayer. We don't add in a section for prayer specifically in the journaling portion of this book, but we strongly encourage you to approach the journal with a prayerful attitude. Be open to interrupting the journal items with a time of prayer, committing things to God as a couple.

WHAT ARE YOU THANKFUL FOR?

Having an attitude of gratitude helps to make your day sweeter and your outlook more positive. It is said that life and death are in the power of the tongue, and those who love it will eat its fruit (Proverbs 18:21). Those that fix their attention and speak life will enjoy the fruit of life! Add thankfulness to your conversations together and see how the tone shifts in your relationship.

WHAT WAS SOMETHING GOOD THAT HAPPENED THIS WEEK?

A week often comprises highs and lows; when we catch up, the most recent event may overshadow other significant events that may have happened. In fact, your brain often pays attention to negative events much more than positive ones (Rozin & Royzman, 2001). Track through your week to find the gold - positive events are like fuel for the soul! They will remind you of the wins you're accumulating in the midst of what might seem like a mundane week. To the listener, feel free to cheer on the speaker as they open up about their victories in the week. Laugh, hug, raise your arms in triumph - this is worth celebrating.

WHAT WAS SOMETHING BAD THAT HAPPENED THIS WEEK?

Even the negative events in life have value. On reflection, most of our growth as a couple have come through incredibly scary, difficult, or painful times together. Our pastor sometimes says that people and events act as dipsticks in an old-school car - they help reveal what is already there and usually aren't the source of the problem. Sometimes our responses to negative events can reveal areas we are insecure about or traumas from the past that we've never revisited. In all negative things we can turn to each other for comfort and solidarity. We are in it for the long haul, so it's time to open up. Share not only the events themselves, but your emotions and thoughts around them. Be open to your husband or wife speaking into that situation, holding your hand, giving you a hug, and standing side-by-side as you face it together. To the listener, this might be a good time to sit and allow the other person to fully express their thoughts and feelings before reacting. Consider praying together regarding any particular insecurities or past traumas - healing is only a prayer away as God allows our minds to be renewed in Him (Romans 12:2).

WHAT ARE YOUR CURRENT HOPES OR DREAMS?

All of us have hopes and dreams. There's no denying that these dreams change their expression through time – this is why it's essential to touch in with each other regarding your dreams and hopes for your lives. I've found this to be a beautiful touch point every week as we remind ourselves of the greater story that we're building with God. It takes my weekly experiences and weaves it into the lifelong journey of faith, lending it fresh purpose and perspective. Sometimes it's as simple as 'I want to listen to you more instead of waiting for my turn to talk'. Sometimes it's as lofty as 'I want God to use me to bring revival to this city'. Voicing out our hopes can help show the desires of our hearts, which helps our husband or wife see the bigger story that's unfolding. Listening to these dreams will help you build a future that converges instead of moves apart.

HOW CAN I BLESS YOU?

Here's a practical one. This is one of the most powerful questions you can ask your spouse. It reminds them that you are there for them and ready to give whatever they need. It challenges both of you to remind yourselves that you are called to love each other, not seek selfish gain (1 Corinthians 13:5). Lastly, it removes the guesswork of having to decipher what might be a good way to touch your husband or wife's heart this week. It can be as simple as 'I'd like 15 minutes of us chatting without distractions every day this week'. It can even look like 'I'd love it if you could hold my hand more.' Now I know you may have your own opinions on how hot your hand feels with their fingers interlaced... but isn't it worth it to see their heart fill up and their smile glowing as you bless them with exactly what they asked for? Let's reflect the great love of Christ towards His church through our marriage relationship (Ephesians 5:22-32).

SEX

This might be one of the most important things to catch up on. How many of us end up going weeks or months without it, which leaves us feeling unfulfilled and frustrated? Sex is crucial in the life of a couple, producing complex reactions in the brain and body (Meston & Fochlich, 2000). Not having sex regularly can decrease a sense of satisfaction in the marriage (Tavakol, Nikbakht Nasrabadi, Behboodi Moghadam, Salehiniya, & Rezaei, 2017). Whether your sexual frequency has been hampered by the hectic schedules you both lead, it's time to invest in sex as the strongest way to strengthen your marriage! Talk about how often you've had sex. Talk about how often you'd like to have sex in a week. Talk about the quality of the sex - how has it been feeling? Both of you have the opportunity to be honest and growth-oriented in making sex better for the both of you!

> **Pro Tip**: putting in calendar events for sexy-time is not boring or weird. It'll probably increase your sex frequency, so schedule those times in!

FINANCES

Let's face it - money is a major issue for couples and financial disagreements are the strongest predictors of divorce (Dew, Britt, & Huston, 2012). We definitely want to avoid divorce... in fact, divorce is something we do not have in our dictionary, so let's make sure we're talking about money. How are we tracking our finances? Do we have enough saved up to cover an emergency expenditure, such as an expensive hospital treatment, a car service, or travelling to a family member who suddenly fell ill? Is there an outstanding credit card balance we should be paying off? How are we going with saving towards our house deposit? If you've ever had these concerns in your mind, here and now is the time to voice them. Financial issues (and how best to tackle them) do not magically go away; make sure you both have formed and communicated a plan to overcome these hurdles together.

IS THERE ANYTHING BOTHERING YOU?

How many of us know someone (or perhaps we're the ones!) who posts on social media about their husband or wife's annoying habits or behaviours? All this energy could be better served by actually talking to the person and working it out! Here's where you talk about the things that bother you. It can be about each other, about work, the emotions you're facing, the prospects of losing your job, or the lack of certainty about the future. This is the time to talk about the things that make you feel bothered - your husband or wife are here to support you, cheer you on, and listen to you. Again, be open to interrupting this or any journal question to pray together. Stand together in your emotions and submit them to the One who is the lifter of our head (Psalm 3:3).

CATCH-UPS

Who are we meeting up with outside of each other? Part of having a healthy marriage is ensuring you are interacting with friends and family - no couple is an island! In fact, one way to build and sustain a sense of resilience to life's challenges is to connect with your broader social context (Rutter, 2012): be it your extended family, school, workplace, or church community. Grow your circles of friendships to make sure you are all supporting each other in times of need! This can be critical in setting up a powerful net personally and for your marriage.

DATE NIGHT

Let's close out this list with a banger. Date night is one of the crucial building blocks of a relationship that married couples throw to the wayside when times get busy - it's so easy to think that you spend so much time together already and you wouldn't need a weekly date time. This couldn't be further from the truth - hey, there's even a book written just so you reinstate a regular date night ('Date Your Wife', Buzzard, 2012)! Do not allow yourself to slip into a state of familiarity and idleness with regard to your marriage. Your husband or wife is a partner and close ally throughout your life, so it's time to start treating them like it. They're also wonderful company! Make sure you go out together. Do a fancy dinner periodically. Try a candlelit picnic at home. Watch a movie together on the couch and give each other massages. Carve out a time together to focus on 'us' and not just the challenges you both have to face. What day and time is date night and what are we doing? Nail down the details, commit to the process, and watch your marriage flourish!

THE END OF
THE BEGINNING

As Sir Winston Churchill, Britain's Prime Minister said at the nation's darkest hour in World War II: "Now this is not the end. It is not even the beginning of the end. But it is, perhaps, the end of the beginning (emphasis added)." The fact that you've picked up this journal and have started this journey represents a new chapter for your marriage. This might not be your relationship's darkest hour. You might simply find that you both want to take this relationship to the next level. That's incredible! For the ones who find that the line of communication between you two has slipped significantly, we pray that your lives would be transformed by the Lord's love for His people. In marriage we find the Father's heart to teach us what love is – it is patient and kind. It does not envy, does not parade itself, is not puffed up. It's not rude or selfish, is not provoked. It thinks no evil. It does not rejoice in iniquity but in the truth. It bears, believes, hopes, and endures all things; it never fails. As you fill the pages of this journal together, we believe that you will find the line of communication reopen between the two of you. Sow into your love weekly and watch it blossom and flourish. We are cheering you on every step of the way!

> [4] **Love suffers long and is kind; love does not envy; love does not parade itself, is not puffed up;** [5] **does not behave rudely, does not seek its own, is not provoked, thinks no evil;** [6] **does not rejoice in iniquity, but rejoices in the truth;** [7] **bears all things, believes all things, hopes all things, endures all things.**
>
> [8] **Love never fails.**
>
> 1 Corinthians 13:4–8 (NKJV)

Now go on to the next pages and let your journaling journey begin!

DATE   /   /

What are you thankful for?

HIM

HER

What was something good that happened this week?

HIM

HER

What was something bad that happened this week?

HIM

HER

What are your current hopes or dreams?

HIM

HER

How can I bless you?

HIM

HER

Sex

HIM _____ HER _____

Finances

HIM _____ HER _____

Is there anything bothering you?

HIM _____ HER _____

Catch-ups

HIM _____ HER _____

Date night

| MON | TUE | WED | THU | FRI | SAT | SUN |

_____

DATE   /   /

What are you thankful for?

HIM

HER

What was something good that happened this week?

HIM

HER

What was something bad that happened this week?

HIM

HER

What are your current hopes or dreams?

HIM

HER

How can I bless you?

HIM

HER

Sex

HIM ....
....

HER ....
....

Finances

HIM ....
....

HER ....
....

Is there anything bothering you?

HIM ....
....

HER ....
....

Catch-ups

HIM ....
....

HER ....
....

Date night

| MON | TUE | WED | THU | FRI | SAT | SUN |

....
....

DATE   /   /

What are you thankful for?

HIM

HER

What was something good that happened this week?

HIM

HER

What was something bad that happened this week?

HIM

HER

What are your current hopes or dreams?

HIM

HER

How can I bless you?

HIM

HER

Sex

HIM .... HER ....

Finances

HIM .... HER ....

Is there anything bothering you?

HIM .... HER ....

Catch-ups

HIM .... HER ....

Date night

MON   TUE   WED   THU   FRI   SAT   SUN

....

Week 4

DATE / /

What are you thankful for?

HIM

HER

What was something good that happened this week?

HIM

HER

What was something bad that happened this week?

HIM

HER

What are your current hopes or dreams?

HIM

HER

How can I bless you?

HIM

HER

Sex

HIM

HER

Finances

HIM

HER

Is there anything bothering you?

HIM

HER

Catch-ups

HIM

HER

Date night

MON   TUE   WED   THU   FRI   SAT   SUN

DATE   /   /

What are you thankful for?

HIM

HER

What was something good that happened this week?

HIM

HER

What was something bad that happened this week?

HIM

HER

What are your current hopes or dreams?

HIM

HER

How can I bless you?

HIM

HER

Sex

HIM

HER

Finances

HIM

HER

Is there anything bothering you?

HIM

HER

Catch-ups

HIM

HER

Date night

MON	TUE	WED	THU	FRI	SAT	SUN

DATE   /   /

What are you thankful for?

HIM

HER

What was something good that happened this week?

HIM

HER

What was something bad that happened this week?

HIM

HER

What are your current hopes or dreams?

HIM

HER

How can I bless you?

HIM

HER

Sex

HIM

HER

Finances

HIM

HER

Is there anything bothering you?

HIM

HER

Catch-ups

HIM

HER

Date night

| MON | TUE | WED | THU | FRI | SAT | SUN |

Week 1

DATE   /   /

What are you thankful for?

HIM

HER

What was something good that happened this week?

HIM

HER

What was something bad that happened this week?

HIM

HER

What are your current hopes or dreams?

HIM

HER

How can I bless you?

HIM

HER

Sex

HIM
....
....
....

HER
....
....
....

Finances

HIM
....
....
....

HER
....
....
....

Is there anything bothering you?

HIM
....
....
....

HER
....
....
....

Catch-ups

HIM
....
....
....

HER
....
....
....

Date night

MON	TUE	WED	THU	FRI	SAT	SUN

....
....

Week 8

DATE / /

What are you thankful for?

HIM

HER

What was something good that happened this week?

HIM

HER

What was something bad that happened this week?

HIM

HER

What are your current hopes or dreams?

HIM

HER

How can I bless you?

HIM

HER

Sex

HIM

HER

Finances

HIM

HER

Is there anything bothering you?

HIM

HER

Catch-ups

HIM

HER

Date night

| MON | TUE | WED | THU | FRI | SAT | SUN |

DATE   /   /

What are you thankful for?

HIM

HER

What was something good that happened this week?

HIM

HER

What was something bad that happened this week?

HIM

HER

What are your current hopes or dreams?

HIM

HER

How can I bless you?

HIM

HER

Sex

HIM

HER

Finances

HIM

HER

Is there anything bothering you?

HIM

HER

Catch-ups

HIM

HER

Date night

| MON | TUE | WED | THU | FRI | SAT | SUN |

Week 10

DATE   /   /

What are you thankful for?

HIM

HER

What was something good that happened this week?

HIM

HER

What was something bad that happened this week?

HIM

HER

What are your current hopes or dreams?

HIM

HER

How can I bless you?

HIM

HER

Sex

HIM

HER

Finances

HIM

HER

Is there anything bothering you?

HIM

HER

Catch-ups

HIM

HER

Date night

| MON | TUE | WED | THU | FRI | SAT | SUN |

Week 11

DATE   /   /

What are you thankful for?

HIM

HER

What was something good that happened this week?

HIM

HER

What was something bad that happened this week?

HIM

HER

What are your current hopes or dreams?

HIM

HER

How can I bless you?

HIM

HER

Sex

HIM

HER

Finances

HIM

HER

Is there anything bothering you?

HIM

HER

Catch-ups

HIM

HER

Date night

MON   TUE   WED   THU   FRI   SAT   SUN

DATE   /   /

What are you thankful for?

HIM

HER

What was something good that happened this week?

HIM

HER

What was something bad that happened this week?

HIM

HER

What are your current hopes or dreams?

HIM

HER

How can I bless you?

HIM

HER

Sex

HIM

HER

Finances

HIM

HER

Is there anything bothering you?

HIM

HER

Catch-ups

HIM

HER

Date night

| MON | TUE | WED | THU | FRI | SAT | SUN |

Week 13

DATE   /   /

What are you thankful for?

HIM

HER

What was something good that happened this week?

HIM

HER

What was something bad that happened this week?

HIM

HER

What are your current hopes or dreams?

HIM

HER

How can I bless you?

HIM

HER

Sex

HIM

HER

Finances

HIM

HER

Is there anything bothering you?

HIM

HER

Catch-ups

HIM

HER

Date night

| MON | TUE | WED | THU | FRI | SAT | SUN |

've# Week 14

DATE   /   /

What are you thankful for?

HIM

HER

What was something good that happened this week?

HIM

HER

What was something bad that happened this week?

HIM

HER

What are your current hopes or dreams?

HIM

HER

How can I bless you?

HIM

HER

Sex

HIM

HER

Finances

HIM

HER

Is there anything bothering you?

HIM

HER

Catch-ups

HIM

HER

Date night

| MON | TUE | WED | THU | FRI | SAT | SUN |

Week 15

DATE   /   /

What are you thankful for?

HIM

HER

What was something good that happened this week?

HIM

HER

What was something bad that happened this week?

HIM

HER

What are your current hopes or dreams?

HIM

HER

How can I bless you?

HIM

HER

Sex

HIM ....

HER ....

Finances

HIM ....

HER ....

Is there anything bothering you?

HIM ....

HER ....

Catch-ups

HIM ....

HER ....

Date night

| MON | TUE | WED | THU | FRI | SAT | SUN |

....

DATE   /   /

What are you thankful for?

HIM

HER

What was something good that happened this week?

HIM

HER

What was something bad that happened this week?

HIM

HER

What are your current hopes or dreams?

HIM

HER

How can I bless you?

HIM

HER

Sex

HIM ....

HER ....

Finances

HIM ....

HER ....

Is there anything bothering you?

HIM ....

HER ....

Catch-ups

HIM ....

HER ....

Date night

| MON | TUE | WED | THU | FRI | SAT | SUN |

Week 17

DATE   /   /

What are you thankful for?

HIM

HER

What was something good that happened this week?

HIM

HER

What was something bad that happened this week?

HIM

HER

What are your current hopes or dreams?

HIM

HER

How can I bless you?

HIM

HER

Sex

HIM

HER

Finances

HIM

HER

Is there anything bothering you?

HIM

HER

Catch-ups

HIM

HER

Date night

| MON | TUE | WED | THU | FRI | SAT | SUN |

DATE / /

What are you thankful for?

HIM

HER

What was something good that happened this week?

HIM

HER

What was something bad that happened this week?

HIM

HER

What are your current hopes or dreams?

HIM

HER

How can I bless you?

HIM

HER

Sex

HIM ....

HER ....

Finances

HIM ....

HER ....

Is there anything bothering you?

HIM ....

HER ....

Catch-ups

HIM ....

HER ....

Date night

| MON | TUE | WED | THU | FRI | SAT | SUN |

Week 19

DATE   /   /

What are you thankful for?

HIM

HER

What was something good that happened this week?

HIM

HER

What was something bad that happened this week?

HIM

HER

What are your current hopes or dreams?

HIM

HER

How can I bless you?

HIM

HER

Sex

HIM

HER

Finances

HIM

HER

Is there anything bothering you?

HIM

HER

Catch-ups

HIM

HER

Date night

| MON | TUE | WED | THU | FRI | SAT | SUN |

DATE   /   /

What are you thankful for?

HIM

HER

What was something good that happened this week?

HIM

HER

What was something bad that happened this week?

HIM

HER

What are your current hopes or dreams?

HIM

HER

How can I bless you?

HIM

HER

Sex

HIM

HER

Finances

HIM

HER

Is there anything bothering you?

HIM

HER

Catch-ups

HIM

HER

Date night

| MON | TUE | WED | THU | FRI | SAT | SUN |

DATE   /   /

What are you thankful for?

HIM

HER

What was something good that happened this week?

HIM

HER

What was something bad that happened this week?

HIM

HER

What are your current hopes or dreams?

HIM

HER

How can I bless you?

HIM

HER

Sex

HIM ....

HER ....

Finances

HIM ....

HER ....

Is there anything bothering you?

HIM ....

HER ....

Catch-ups

HIM ....

HER ....

Date night

| MON | TUE | WED | THU | FRI | SAT | SUN |

....

Week 22

DATE   /   /

What are you thankful for?

HIM

HER

What was something good that happened this week?

HIM

HER

What was something bad that happened this week?

HIM

HER

What are your current hopes or dreams?

HIM

HER

How can I bless you?

HIM

HER

Sex

HIM

HER

Finances

HIM

HER

Is there anything bothering you?

HIM

HER

Catch-ups

HIM

HER

Date night

| MON | TUE | WED | THU | FRI | SAT | SUN |

DATE / /

What are you thankful for?

HIM

HER

What was something good that happened this week?

HIM

HER

What was something bad that happened this week?

HIM

HER

What are your current hopes or dreams?

HIM

HER

How can I bless you?

HIM

HER

Sex

HIM

HER

Finances

HIM

HER

Is there anything bothering you?

HIM

HER

Catch-ups

HIM

HER

Date night

| MON | TUE | WED | THU | FRI | SAT | SUN |

DATE   /   /

What are you thankful for?

HIM

HER

What was something good that happened this week?

HIM

HER

What was something bad that happened this week?

HIM

HER

What are your current hopes or dreams?

HIM

HER

How can I bless you?

HIM

HER

Sex

HIM .... HER ....
....

Finances

HIM .... HER ....
....

Is there anything bothering you?

HIM .... HER ....
....

Catch-ups

HIM .... HER ....
....

Date night

MON	TUE	WED	THU	FRI	SAT	SUN

....
....

DATE / /

What are you thankful for?

HIM

HER

What was something good that happened this week?

HIM

HER

What was something bad that happened this week?

HIM

HER

What are your current hopes or dreams?

HIM

HER

How can I bless you?

HIM

HER

Sex

HIM

HER

Finances

HIM

HER

Is there anything bothering you?

HIM

HER

Catch-ups

HIM

HER

Date night

| MON | TUE | WED | THU | FRI | SAT | SUN |

DATE   /   /

What are you thankful for?

HIM

HER

What was something good that happened this week?

HIM

HER

What was something bad that happened this week?

HIM

HER

What are your current hopes or dreams?

HIM

HER

How can I bless you?

HIM

HER

Sex

HIM .... HER ....

Finances

HIM .... HER ....

Is there anything bothering you?

HIM .... HER ....

Catch-ups

HIM .... HER ....

Date night

| MON | TUE | WED | THU | FRI | SAT | SUN |

....

DATE   /   /

What are you thankful for?

HIM

HER

What was something good that happened this week?

HIM

HER

What was something bad that happened this week?

HIM

HER

What are your current hopes or dreams?

HIM

HER

How can I bless you?

HIM

HER

Sex

HIM

HER

Finances

HIM

HER

Is there anything bothering you?

HIM

HER

Catch-ups

HIM

HER

Date night

| MON | TUE | WED | THU | FRI | SAT | SUN |

# Week 28

DATE / /

What are you thankful for?

HIM

HER

What was something good that happened this week?

HIM

HER

What was something bad that happened this week?

HIM

HER

What are your current hopes or dreams?

HIM

HER

How can I bless you?

HIM

HER

Sex

HIM .... HER ....

Finances

HIM .... HER ....

Is there anything bothering you?

HIM .... HER ....

Catch-ups

HIM .... HER ....

Date night

| MON | TUE | WED | THU | FRI | SAT | SUN |

DATE   /   /

What are you thankful for?

HIM

HER

What was something good that happened this week?

HIM

HER

What was something bad that happened this week?

HIM

HER

What are your current hopes or dreams?

HIM

HER

How can I bless you?

HIM

HER

Sex

HIM

HER

Finances

HIM

HER

Is there anything bothering you?

HIM

HER

Catch-ups

HIM

HER

Date night

| MON | TUE | WED | THU | FRI | SAT | SUN |

DATE   /   /

What are you thankful for?

HIM

HER

What was something good that happened this week?

HIM

HER

What was something bad that happened this week?

HIM

HER

What are your current hopes or dreams?

HIM

HER

How can I bless you?

HIM

HER

Sex

HIM

HER

Finances

HIM

HER

Is there anything bothering you?

HIM

HER

Catch-ups

HIM

HER

Date night

| MON | TUE | WED | THU | FRI | SAT | SUN |

Week 31

DATE / /

What are you thankful for?

HIM

HER

What was something good that happened this week?

HIM

HER

What was something bad that happened this week?

HIM

HER

What are your current hopes or dreams?

HIM

HER

How can I bless you?

HIM

HER

Sex

HIM

HER

Finances

HIM

HER

Is there anything bothering you?

HIM

HER

Catch-ups

HIM

HER

Date night

| MON | TUE | WED | THU | FRI | SAT | SUN |

DATE   /   /

What are you thankful for?

HIM

HER

What was something good that happened this week?

HIM

HER

What was something bad that happened this week?

HIM

HER

What are your current hopes or dreams?

HIM

HER

How can I bless you?

HIM

HER

Sex

HIM

HER

Finances

HIM

HER

Is there anything bothering you?

HIM

HER

Catch-ups

HIM

HER

Date night

| MON | TUE | WED | THU | FRI | SAT | SUN |

Week 33

DATE / /

What are you thankful for?

HIM

HER

What was something good that happened this week?

HIM

HER

What was something bad that happened this week?

HIM

HER

What are your current hopes or dreams?

HIM

HER

How can I bless you?

HIM

HER

Sex

HIM

HER

Finances

HIM

HER

Is there anything bothering you?

HIM

HER

Catch-ups

HIM

HER

Date night

MON	TUE	WED	THU	FRI	SAT	SUN

Week 34

DATE / /

What are you thankful for?

HIM

HER

What was something good that happened this week?

HIM

HER

What was something bad that happened this week?

HIM

HER

What are your current hopes or dreams?

HIM

HER

How can I bless you?

HIM

HER

Sex

HIM

HER

Finances

HIM

HER

Is there anything bothering you?

HIM

HER

Catch-ups

HIM

HER

Date night

| MON | TUE | WED | THU | FRI | SAT | SUN |

DATE   /   /

What are you thankful for?

HIM

HER

What was something good that happened this week?

HIM

HER

What was something bad that happened this week?

HIM

HER

What are your current hopes or dreams?

HIM

HER

How can I bless you?

HIM

HER

Sex

HIM ....

HER ....

Finances

HIM ....

HER ....

Is there anything bothering you?

HIM ....

HER ....

Catch-ups

HIM ....

HER ....

Date night

| MON | TUE | WED | THU | FRI | SAT | SUN |

....
....

Week 36

DATE / /

What are you thankful for?

HIM

HER

What was something good that happened this week?

HIM

HER

What was something bad that happened this week?

HIM

HER

What are your current hopes or dreams?

HIM

HER

How can I bless you?

HIM

HER

Sex

HIM

HER

Finances

HIM

HER

Is there anything bothering you?

HIM

HER

Catch-ups

HIM

HER

Date night

| MON | TUE | WED | THU | FRI | SAT | SUN |

Week 31

DATE   /   /

What are you thankful for?

HIM

HER

What was something good that happened this week?

HIM

HER

What was something bad that happened this week?

HIM

HER

What are your current hopes or dreams?

HIM

HER

How can I bless you?

HIM

HER

Sex

HIM

HER

Finances

HIM

HER

Is there anything bothering you?

HIM

HER

Catch-ups

HIM

HER

Date night

| MON | TUE | WED | THU | FRI | SAT | SUN |

DATE   /   /

What are you thankful for?

HIM

HER

What was something good that happened this week?

HIM

HER

What was something bad that happened this week?

HIM

HER

What are your current hopes or dreams?

HIM

HER

How can I bless you?

HIM

HER

Sex

HIM

HER

Finances

HIM

HER

Is there anything bothering you?

HIM

HER

Catch-ups

HIM

HER

Date night

MON	TUE	WED	THU	FRI	SAT	SUN

Week 39

DATE / /

What are you thankful for?

HIM

HER

What was something good that happened this week?

HIM

HER

What was something bad that happened this week?

HIM

HER

What are your current hopes or dreams?

HIM

HER

How can I bless you?

HIM

HER

Sex

HIM

HER

Finances

HIM

HER

Is there anything bothering you?

HIM

HER

Catch-ups

HIM

HER

Date night

| MON | TUE | WED | THU | FRI | SAT | SUN |

DATE   /   /

What are you thankful for?

HIM

HER

What was something good that happened this week?

HIM

HER

What was something bad that happened this week?

HIM

HER

What are your current hopes or dreams?

HIM

HER

How can I bless you?

HIM

HER

Sex

HIM

HER

Finances

HIM

HER

Is there anything bothering you?

HIM

HER

Catch-ups

HIM

HER

Date night

MON	TUE	WED	THU	FRI	SAT	SUN

Week 41

DATE   /   /

What are you thankful for?

HIM

HER

What was something good that happened this week?

HIM

HER

What was something bad that happened this week?

HIM

HER

What are your current hopes or dreams?

HIM

HER

How can I bless you?

HIM

HER

Sex

HIM

HER

Finances

HIM

HER

Is there anything bothering you?

HIM

HER

Catch-ups

HIM

HER

Date night

MON   TUE   WED   THU   FRI   SAT   SUN

DATE   /   /

What are you thankful for?

HIM

HER

What was something good that happened this week?

HIM

HER

What was something bad that happened this week?

HIM

HER

What are your current hopes or dreams?

HIM

HER

How can I bless you?

HIM

HER

Sex

HIM ....

HER ....

Finances

HIM ....

HER ....

Is there anything bothering you?

HIM ....

HER ....

Catch-ups

HIM ....

HER ....

Date night

| MON | TUE | WED | THU | FRI | SAT | SUN |

Week 43

DATE   /   /

What are you thankful for?

HIM

HER

What was something good that happened this week?

HIM

HER

What was something bad that happened this week?

HIM

HER

What are your current hopes or dreams?

HIM

HER

How can I bless you?

HIM

HER

Sex

HIM ....
....
....

HER ....
....
....

Finances

HIM ....
....
....

HER ....
....
....

Is there anything bothering you?

HIM ....
....
....

HER ....
....
....

Catch-ups

HIM ....
....
....

HER ....
....
....

Date night

MON	TUE	WED	THU	FRI	SAT	SUN

....
....

DATE   /   /

What are you thankful for?

HIM

HER

What was something good that happened this week?

HIM

HER

What was something bad that happened this week?

HIM

HER

What are your current hopes or dreams?

HIM

HER

How can I bless you?

HIM

HER

Sex

HIM ....

HER ....

Finances

HIM ....

HER ....

Is there anything bothering you?

HIM ....

HER ....

Catch-ups

HIM ....

HER ....

Date night

MON	TUE	WED	THU	FRI	SAT	SUN

DATE   /   /

What are you thankful for?

HIM

HER

What was something good that happened this week?

HIM

HER

What was something bad that happened this week?

HIM

HER

What are your current hopes or dreams?

HIM

HER

How can I bless you?

HIM

HER

Sex

HIM

HER

Finances

HIM

HER

Is there anything bothering you?

HIM

HER

Catch-ups

HIM

HER

Date night

| MON | TUE | WED | THU | FRI | SAT | SUN |

DATE   /   /

What are you thankful for?

HIM

HER

What was something good that happened this week?

HIM

HER

What was something bad that happened this week?

HIM

HER

What are your current hopes or dreams?

HIM

HER

How can I bless you?

HIM

HER

Sex

HIM

HER

Finances

HIM

HER

Is there anything bothering you?

HIM

HER

Catch-ups

HIM

HER

Date night

| MON | TUE | WED | THU | FRI | SAT | SUN |

DATE   /   /

What are you thankful for?

HIM .... HER ....

What was something good that happened this week?

HIM .... HER ....

What was something bad that happened this week?

HIM .... HER ....

What are your current hopes or dreams?

HIM .... HER ....

How can I bless you?

HIM .... HER ....

Sex

HIM

HER

Finances

HIM

HER

Is there anything bothering you?

HIM

HER

Catch-ups

HIM

HER

Date night

| MON | TUE | WED | THU | FRI | SAT | SUN |

DATE / /

What are you thankful for?

HIM

HER

What was something good that happened this week?

HIM

HER

What was something bad that happened this week?

HIM

HER

What are your current hopes or dreams?

HIM

HER

How can I bless you?

HIM

HER

Sex

HIM

HER

Finances

HIM

HER

Is there anything bothering you?

HIM

HER

Catch-ups

HIM

HER

Date night

| MON | TUE | WED | THU | FRI | SAT | SUN |

DATE   /   /

What are you thankful for?

HIM

HER

What was something good that happened this week?

HIM

HER

What was something bad that happened this week?

HIM

HER

What are your current hopes or dreams?

HIM

HER

How can I bless you?

HIM

HER

Sex

HIM

HER

Finances

HIM

HER

Is there anything bothering you?

HIM

HER

Catch-ups

HIM

HER

Date night

| MON | TUE | WED | THU | FRI | SAT | SUN |

DATE / /

What are you thankful for?

HIM

HER

What was something good that happened this week?

HIM

HER

What was something bad that happened this week?

HIM

HER

What are your current hopes or dreams?

HIM

HER

How can I bless you?

HIM

HER

Sex

HIM ....

HER ....

Finances

HIM ....

HER ....

Is there anything bothering you?

HIM ....

HER ....

Catch-ups

HIM ....

HER ....

Date night

MON	TUE	WED	THU	FRI	SAT	SUN

Week 51

DATE   /   /

What are you thankful for?

HIM

HER

What was something good that happened this week?

HIM

HER

What was something bad that happened this week?

HIM

HER

What are your current hopes or dreams?

HIM

HER

How can I bless you?

HIM

HER

Sex

HIM

HER

Finances

HIM

HER

Is there anything bothering you?

HIM

HER

Catch-ups

HIM

HER

Date night

| MON | TUE | WED | THU | FRI | SAT | SUN |

DATE   /   /

What are you thankful for?

HIM

HER

What was something good that happened this week?

HIM

HER

What was something bad that happened this week?

HIM

HER

What are your current hopes or dreams?

HIM

HER

How can I bless you?

HIM

HER

Sex

HIM

HER

Finances

HIM

HER

Is there anything bothering you?

HIM

HER

Catch-ups

HIM

HER

Date night

MON	TUE	WED	THU	FRI	SAT	SUN

REFERENCES

Buzzard, J. (2012). Date Your Wife. Crossway. Cambridge University Press. (2022, April 6). TRIUMPHANT | meaning in the Cambridge English Dictionary. Cambridge Dictionary. Retrieved April 12, 2022, from https://dictionary.cambridge.org/dictionary/english/triumphant

Dew, J., Britt, S., & Huston, S. (2012). Examining the relationship between financial issues and divorce. Family Relations, 61(4), 615-628. https://doi.org/10.1111/j.1741-3729.2012.00715.x

Jain, S. (2008, July 23). 4102.0 - Australian Social Trends, 2007. Australian Bureau of Statistics. Retrieved April 12, 2022, from https://www.abs.gov.au/ausstats/abs.nsf/0/26D94B4C9A4769E6CA25732C00207644?opendocument#DIVORCE

Meston, C. M., & Frohlich, P. F. (2000). The neurobiology of sexual function. Archives of General Psychiatry, 57(11), 1012-1030. https://jamanetwork.com/journals/jamapsychiatry/article-abstract/481665

Norcross, J. C., & Vangarelli, D. J. (1999). The resolution solution: Longitudinal examination of New Year's change attempts. Journal of substance abuse, 1(2), 127-134. https://doi.org/10.1016/S0899-3289(88)80016-6

Rozin, P., & Royzman, E. B. (2001). *Negativity bias, negativity dominance, and contagion. Personality and social psychology review,* 5(4), 296-320.
https://doi.org/10.1207/S15327957PSPR0504_2

Rutter, M. (2012). *Resilience: Causal pathways and social ecology. In M. Ungar (Ed.), The Social Ecology of Resilience: A Handbook of Theory and Practice* (pp. 33-42). Springer.
https://link.springer.com/chapter/10.1007/978-1-4614-0586-3_3

Sillars, A. L., Pike, G. R., Jones, T. C., & Murphy, M. A. (1984, March). *Communication and understanding in marriage. Human Communication Research,* 10(3), 317-350.
https://doi.org/10.1111/j.1468-2958.1984.tb00022.x

Tavakol, Z., Nikbakht Nasrabadi, A., Behboodi Moghadam, Z., Salehiniya, H., & Rezaei, E. (2017). *A review of the factors associated with marital satisfaction. Galen Medical Journal,* 6(3).http://eprints.skums.ac.ir/6056/

Zetter, K. (2015, August 18). *Hackers Finally Post Stolen Ashley Madison Data.* WIRED. Retrieved April 12, 2022, from
https://www.wired.com/2015/08/happened-hackers-posted-stolen-ashley-madison-data/

www.ingramcontent.com/pod-product-compliance
Lightning Source LLC
Chambersburg PA
CBHW070307010526
44107CB00056B/2514